LIFE ON THE EDGE

AMAZING ANIMAL ANATOMIES

BIOLOGY AT ITS MOST EXTREME!

CHERITON
CHILDREN'S BOOKS

Published in 2023 by **Cheriton Children's Books**
1 Bank Drive West, Shrewsbury, Shropshire, SY3 9DJ, UK

First Edition

Authors: Kelly Roberts and Louise Spilsbury
Designer: Paul Myerscough
Editor: Louisa Simmons
Proofreader: Jessica Edwards

Picture credits: Cover: Shutterstock/Tomatito; Inside: p1: Shutterstock/Acceptphoto; p4: Shutterstock/Beth Ruggiero-York; p5: Shutterstock/Sebastian Janicki; p6: Shutterstock/Lukas Jonaitis; p7: Shutterstock/Snow Hana; p8: Shutterstock/Kristina Postnikova; p9: Shutterstock/Brian Lasenby; p10: Shutterstock/Adam Wildlife; p11: Shutterstock/Kurit Afshen; p12: Shutterstock/EcoPrint; p13: Shutterstock/Ernie Cooper; p14: Shutterstock/Rene Mayorga; p15: Shutterstock/Tran The Ngoc; p16: Shutterstock/Saraporn; p17: Shutterstock/Kjersti Joergensen; p18: Shutterstock/J.T. Lewis; p19: Shutterstock/Acceptphoto; p20: Shutterstock/Tomas Kotouc; p21: Shutterstock/Frantisekhojdysz; p22: Shutterstock/K A Studio; p23: Shutterstock/Vladimir Wrangel; p24: Shutterstock/Audrey Snider-Bell; p25: Shutterstock/Aastels; p26: Shutterstock/Dwi Yulianto; p27: Shutterstock/Matt Cornish; p28: Shutterstock/Wright Out There; p29: Shutterstock/Chris Watson; p30: Shutterstock/Agami Photo Agency; p31: Shutterstock/Flipser; p32: Shutterstock/Marek Mihulka; p33: Shutterstock/Vaclav Sebek; p34: Shutterstock/Juan Diego Quintero Urrea; p35: Shutterstock/Pagina; p36: Shutterstock/Robin Scholte; p37: Shutterstock/Sourabh Bharti; p38: Shutterstock/Sagar Gosavi Photography; p39: Shutterstock/Juergen Wallstabe; p40: Shutterstock/Henner Damke; p41: Shutterstock/Esdeem; p42: Shutterstock/Rudmer Zwerver; p43: Shutterstock/Natalia Golovina; p44: Shutterstock/Yakov Oskanov; p45: Shutterstock/Ryan Boedi.

Printed in China

WHAT'S ON THE COVER?

The jumping spider uses its amazing eyesight to hunt down prey.

Page 1: a porcupine pufferfish (see page 19).

CONTENTS

CHAPTER 1

AMAZING INSECTS

From elephants and humans, to birds and snakes, there is a huge variety of **species** on Earth, and each one has a very special anatomy, or shape and arrangement of body parts. Some animals, such as chimpanzees, have anatomies that are familiar to us and similar to our own, but others look very strange!

Bats have wide wings that help them fly and sharp teeth for eating food.

Shaped for Survival

Strange though animal anatomies can seem, every part of them has a function that contributes to survival. Anatomies are the result of millions of years of gradual change in **organisms**—a process in which mechanisms that work are perfected, and those that do not are lost. For example, if a bat's wings or teeth did not work properly, it would not be able to catch **insects** to eat. Parts of an anatomy are also interconnected, for example, if we did not have skeletons, our muscles would not work and we would collapse. Insects do not have skeletons, but they have tough casings, called **exoskeletons**, for support.

Features of a Fly

Most insects are so small that their unusual features are extremely difficult to see. For example, the common housefly slurps up its food with a sponge-like mouth, has feet that can smell, and is equipped with up to 6,000 eyes that can sense light and dark. Its amazing eyes are grouped together so they create an all-around view of the fly's world.

BRUTAL BIOLOGY

Have you ever heard a housefly's buzzing noise? It is created when the fly beats its two wings up to 300 times a second! The flies also have two tiny dumbbell-shaped stumps that beat in time with the wings. The weights act as stabilizers so the insect can safely fly.

Flies and most adult insects have enormous eyes that help them see the world around them.

Cartoon Caterpillar!

When seen up-close, a puss moth caterpillar has a very unusual appearance—a round face, a large nose and black eyes, and two twirling black tails! This unusual creature may look strange, but its appearance has a purpose.

Putting on a Show

The puss moth caterpillar puts on a show to keep would-be **predators** away. The orange ring and black eyes on its face make the caterpillar look more threatening than it really is. It looks even scarier when it swings its head from side to side. Then, for even greater effect, bright-red whips emerge from the caterpillar's tails and wave about, and if the caterpillar is threatened, the tails give off liquid that stings a predator's eyes.

The puss moth caterpillar has an extraordinary head.

This caterpillar is green to **camouflage** it against leaves.

All Change

When the puss moth caterpillar is ready to turn into a moth, its color changes to orange, and then purple. Next, it spins a covering of silk and bark around itself. It stays in this **cocoon** over winter, changing all the time. Many parts of its body dissolve, and then re-form into a flying adult animal. This is called **metamorphosis**. The moth that emerges is covered with soft fur, a little like that on a cat —which gives the insect its name, puss moth.

BRUTAL BIOLOGY

Many caterpillars are covered with hairs and while they may look cute, you should never touch them! Caterpillars are often armed with a secret weapon. For example, the southern flannel moth caterpillar is covered with long, fine, tan-colored hairs. They easily stick into skin and break. When they do so, they release a chemical that causes itching, burning, rashes, and sickness. No wonder predators keep away!

Pray It Stays Away!

The mantis may appear to be praying, but there is nothing peaceful about this predator! Its enormous, spiked front legs are lethal weapons, and its huge eyes scan the horizon for food.

A praying mantis loves to eat and may gulp down up to 16 crickets a day!

Headfirst Hunter

A mantis looks out for **prey**, standing quietly with its legs spread out and its head lifted high. When it spots prey, it moves its head from side to side. It carefully tracks its prey, then when it is within reach, the mantis strikes. Its front legs shoot forward with lightning speed, and stab into the prey. The mantis usually eats an animal headfirst with its tough jaws, yum!

Fierce Female

Mantises attack almost anything that moves, including insects, frogs, mice, and even birds. No wonder the males approach female mantises carefully when it is time to **mate**! A hungry female may even eat a male that tries to mate with her! Mantises may be fierce, but they are at risk of being eaten themselves by larger predators, such as birds. For that reason, mantises are camouflaged in natural colors, such as green. That helps them blend in with the leaves and flowers among which they wait for prey.

BRUTAL BIOLOGY

The mantis has an awesome relative—the walking stick. This stick insect is the longest insect in the world. It measures an amazing 21 inches (53 cm) long and looks like one of the branches it hides on. Its body is designed to hide the insect from predators.

Stick insects look just like the sticks they crawl across.

CHAPTER 2

EIGHT-LEGGED HUNTERS

Spiders and scorpions are fearsome predators. These smart hunters have amazing anatomies to help them catch prey. Adaptable spiders can live in almost any environment on Earth, while scorpions are usually found only in dry, hot areas.

Super-Scary Spider

The tarantula has a reputation for sending shivers down the spine, and for good reason—the creature looks super-scary! Unlike some spiders, tarantulas do not weave webs to catch prey, but instead hunt at night. They use the sensitive hairs all over their bodies and legs to feel vibrations made by small animals such as grasshoppers, frogs, toads, and mice. The spiders then follow the vibrations to sneak up on animals and eat them!

Tarantulas release tiny, almost invisible hairs from their legs that sting any predators that threaten them.

Slurping Spider!

When a tarantula pounces on an unsuspecting victim, it bites into it with its large fangs. It uses its legs to keep a firm grip on the prey. The fangs deliver a deadly dose of **venom**, which is a poison. The venom juices turn the prey into a soup that the hungry spider can slurp.

Hundreds of different species of tarantulas can be found around the world.

BRUTAL BIOLOGY

The goliath bird-eating spider is so-named because it is huge! It is large enough to catch and eat birds. The spider has fangs that are almost 1 inch (2.5 cm) long, and it uses them to inject its victims with venom. It is also the heaviest tarantula in the world, and can weigh up to 6 ounces (175 g).

Sting in the Tail

A scorpion can be easily spotted. It has two enormous pincers at the front of its body and a long, curving tail with a stinger at the tip. The scorpion is designed to be dangerous, and it is armed to kill.

Pincer Pinch

A scorpion's large front pincers are hard and very strong. The creature uses them to kill prey and defend itself. A scorpion catches prey in different ways—it may chase it or lie in wait for a passing victim. When the scorpion spots its dinner, it darts forward, grabs the animal, and crushes and kills it. If crushing is not enough, the scorpion uses its pincers to hold prey still while its tail delivers a deadly sting.

A scorpion uses its legs to chase after prey.

Toxic Tail

The scorpion's tail is made up of different sections. That is so it can curl up and uncurl easily. In the stinger at the end of the tail is a pair of **glands** that contain poison. The deadly mixture is powerful enough to kill small animals and stun large prey. It takes a lot of energy to make more venom, which is why scorpions use their stingers only when they have to.

BRUTAL BIOLOGY

Some scorpions have stingers that produce two types of venom. One is lethal and can kill. The other only stuns prey. These scorpions create a venom that can tackle large predators, such as owls and coyotes.

Spider Jump

Jumping spiders are so-named because they can jump incredibly high. In fact, they can leap more than 50 times their own body length! These star spiders also have another amazing attribute —the rows of big eyes perched on the front of their heads.

Lunchtime Leaper

Jumping spiders sneak up on insects and other **invertebrates**. Then, when they are close enough, they leap into the air. Next, they land on their victims. Lastly, they inject them with venom to kill them. The spiders also have another trick—when they jump up or down, they release threads of silk that attach the spiders to a surface. That keeps them from falling if they miss their targets.

Jumping spiders inject their prey with venom.

Having different eyes in rows gives the jumping spider amazing eyesight.

Night Sight

Most spiders have poor eyesight, but not the jumping spider. It uses its amazing vision to hunt down its prey. The spider has two big eyes on the front of its head and four smaller eyes on top. The two big eyes can see objects up to 12 inches (30 cm) away. While the smaller eyes do not see as sharply, they help the spiders see farther away.

BRUTAL BIOLOGY

A male jumping spider knows how to impress a female—he can crouch, bob, dance, and even sing! He uses his back legs to send sounds that vibrate on the surface he stands on. Any nearby female can feel the vibrations, but the male must hope that the female is impressed—if not, she will eat him!

CHAPTER 3

DESIGNED FOR WATER

Earth is a watery planet—almost three-quarters of it is covered by oceans. Inside these watery worlds live almost half of the world's species, including jellyfish, sharks, whales, starfish, and squid.

Ocean Life

Many animals that live in oceans have unusual bodies to help them survive in their water worlds. For example, the deep-sea gulper eel has lights that lure prey close. It also has a huge mouth, far bigger than its body, which can swallow any size of prey. Jellyfish have remarkable anatomies, from the bell-shaped bodies that help keep them afloat to their trailing **tentacles**, which are armed with stingers to catch prey.

*A jellyfish's tentacles contain stinging cells that can **paralyze** prey.*

Leafy Life

Some ocean anatomies are designed for hiding. An example is the mussel, which has a shell that hides its body. The leafy sea dragon, a type of sea horse, also hides to keep safe from predators. It does so by looking exactly like a piece of seaweed! It uses its **fins** to move very slowly and almost invisibly among seaweeds, sucking in tiny shrimp and fish larvae as it goes.

The leafy parts on a leafy sea dragon's body look just like seaweed!

BRUTAL BIOLOGY

Male sea horses can do something that very few other male animals can do—they can become pregnant! The male becomes pregnant when a female lays eggs in a special pouch on its stomach. This pouch swells, protecting up to 1,000 eggs as they develop. When the baby sea horses hatch inside the pouch, the male twists and bends to make the pouch split open. Then, the youngsters swim away.

Porcupine pufferfish can reach 30 inches (76 cm) long.

All Puffed Up

The porcupine pufferfish has a unique look. Even when it is relaxed, the animal has bulging eyes, a big mouth, a square head, and is covered with spines. But when it is scared, it starts to look really spooky—it puffs up into a spiky ball!

Spiny and Swollen

The warm **tropical** waters where porcupine pufferfish live are full of fish, and they are all on the look-out for food. The poor pufferfish is not a great swimmer, so it needs another tactic to get away from prey—fear. To scare off predators, the pufferfish pumps huge volumes of water, or sometimes air, into its stomach. The stomach is pleated and elastic, so it can expand far beyond its normal size. The fish swells up, forcing its spines to stick out —surprising any predators watching. They weren't expecting their prey to get bigger, and bigger, and bigger—and spikier!

Toxic Terror

The pufferfish contains a lethal poison called tetrodotoxin, which is about 1,000 times more deadly than cyanide. If any animal does eat the fish, it will be paralyzed and die within 30 minutes. The only fish that are unaffected by the poison are some types of sharks.

BRUTAL BIOLOGY

In Japan, some people eat pufferfish in special restaurants. There, highly trained chefs cut up the pufferfish into pieces to eat without damaging the organs that contain the poison, so the fish is safe to eat.

Porcupine pufferfish can expand to three times their normal size in seconds.

Shaped Like a Hammer

The hammerhead shark is one of the most unusual-looking creatures on Earth. It has eyes spread wide apart on a flat, wing-shaped head called a cephalofoil. The shark's head looks a little like a hammer, which is how it got its name.

Side Eyes

While it may look strange, the head of the shark has a purpose —to find prey. The shark moves its head from side to side in the water, all the while searching for food. The widely spaced eyes allow the hammerhead to judge water depth and distance better than many other sharks. Sharks can smell blood and other traces of prey very well, but the hammerhead's well-spread nostrils give it an even greater sense of smell. **Sensory pits** across the underside of the head can detect electricity made by moving animals, including stingrays that are hiding beneath sand on the seafloor. And when the shark finds its prey, it strikes—just like a hammer.

Hammerheads often swim in large groups of sharks, called schools.

Hammerhead sharks love to eat stingrays.

Terrifying Teeth

Hammerheads have rows of sharp teeth, and when front teeth wear down or fall out, new teeth are ready to take their place. Some small hammerheads, called bonnetheads, have rounded cephalofoils that are shaped like the head of a shovel. They also have blunt back teeth. They use them to grind through tough crab shells before sucking out the meat inside.

BRUTAL BIOLOGY

Remora are fish that cling onto sharks using sucker-shaped fins on their backs. These fish save effort by doing this, and also get to feed on scraps of flesh dropped in the water by the sharks.

Octopuses often drop down on their prey from above.

Eight-Armed Wonder

An octopus is one of the world's wonders. It has eight long arms, each lined with two rows of suckers, and they all reach out from just below the octopus's eyes!

Camouflage King

The skin of an octopus has thousands of tiny sacs, or pouches, of ink. They help the octopus quickly change color. The sacs can shift around in a split second to give the skin the exact color and pattern of the sand or rocks the octopus is resting on. If a predator is not fooled by this camouflage, the octopus simply empties the contents of an ink sac from behind its head into the water. It then escapes, leaving its inky cloud behind.

Shapeshifter

Octopuses do not have skeletons. They have soft bodies, and use their muscles to change shape. They can squeeze into tiny spaces to escape from predators or to find prey. An octopus can also change its body to look like a scary animal, to deter predators. For example, it swims with its arms held out stiffly to mimic the fins of the poisonous lionfish. It also buries itself in the sand and wiggles two arms to look like a sea snake!

BRUTAL BIOLOGY

An octopus has a sharp, horny beak and a tongue that is coated with sharp lumps. It uses the beak and tongue to grind open crab and clam shells and scrape out the flesh inside. Octopus saliva is poisonous—it can paralyze prey, allowing the octopus to feed on it without a struggle.

Octopuses can change color depending on how they feel. They turn red when angry or white if frightened.

CHAPTER 4

REMARKABLE REPTILES

Reptiles are a class of animals. The class is made up of four groups that are very different in appearance, but are all scaly **vertebrates** that lay eggs on land.

A Deadly Group

Iguanas, geckos, and skinks are all types of lizards. They are the most common group of reptiles. They usually have four limbs, long bodies, and tails. Crocodiles are huge reptiles with long, toothed jaws and heavily armored skin. The other types of reptiles are very different. Turtles and tortoises have giant bony shells on their backs to protect their bodies. Snakes have long bodies, short tails, and no legs. Some snakes, such as rattlesnakes, kill prey by injecting venom through grooves in their sharp fangs, while others kill without venom.

Crocodiles swallow stones that grind up food inside their stomachs.

Pythons, such as this green tree python, have camouflaged skin which helps them ambush prey. They can also eat animals much bigger than themselves.

Super Snakes

Pythons are among the longest snakes in the world! They grow to lengths of up to 20 feet (6 m). Pythons kill prey by coiling their muscular bodies around their victims and squeezing tightly until the animals cannot breathe. The snakes are called **constrictors**, because they constrict prey. Once a python's prey is dead and not moving, the snake uncoils. It then opens its upper jaw wide enough to swallow its meal whole. The snake ripples its muscles to pull the prey slowly into its stomach, and **digests** the food over days or even weeks. Pythons have special tubes leading from their lungs to their mouths, which stay open even when the snakes are swallowing food. That keeps the animals from suffocating.

BRUTAL BIOLOGY

Pythons have sensory pits along their jaws, which can sense the heat given off by any **warm-blooded** mammals nearby. That helps the snakes find prey in the dark.

All a Show

The frilled lizard has one of the most extreme animal anatomies in Australia. Now, that is quite an achievement for a country full of amazing animals! The lizard has an enormous frill around its head that is as wide as the animal is long. When the lizard opens the frill, it looks big and scary. That helps it frighten off any predators.

Feeling Frilly

The lizard's neck frill is a large piece of loose, pleated skin that usually flops around its shoulders. When the animal is irritated or threatened, it quickly raises and opens the frill so that it looks about four times larger than it really is. At the same time, the frilled lizard opens its brightly colored mouth wide and lets out a loud hiss. The scary sight and sound is enough to scare away most predators.

The frill on the frilled lizard measures up to 12 inches (30 cm) across.

To avoid predators, frilled lizards mainly stay in the trees.

Lizard Leaper

The frilled lizard spends most of its time clinging to trees. There it can scan the ground for insects or small mammals to eat. When it spots a meal, the lizard leaps down to the ground and runs along on its back legs to catch it. Few lizards can run far on two legs, because they would topple over. However, the frilled lizard has a smart way to keep its balance, even when running fast—it pulls its upper body back, until its head is over its back legs.

BRUTAL BIOLOGY

The frilled lizard has a smart way to avoid trouble while resting in trees. It plays hide-and-seek! If a larger lizard or another predator approaches, it moves to the opposite side of the tree trunk. If the predator starts to walk around the bottom of the tree, the frilled lizard dodges around the trunk.

Desert Devil

The thorny devil sounds like a scary beast. It looks like one too, because its body is covered with sharp, thorn-like spikes. However, this desert lizard isn't scary at all—it spends its days peacefully, just moving across the sand, searching for a meal.

Thorny Hider

One reason why the thorny devil is covered in spikes is to protect it from predators. It also has a range of sandy colors on its back to help it blend in with its desert habitat. Thorny devils are able to keep very still in times of danger, which helps them hide from predators. If a predator does attack, the lizard's super-sharp spikes are enough to stop most animals taking a bite!

The largest of the thorny devil's spines stick out from its snout and over each eye.

Soak It Up

The cone-shaped, sharp spikes also stop the thorny devil from getting too thirsty in the dry desert. Between the spines there are grooves where droplets of morning dew and water from damp sand collect all over the lizard's body. The water then flows along the grooves and into the lizard's mouth.

Thorny devils may move slowly but they can travel up to 980 feet (300 m) a day across the fiercely hot Australian desert where the lizards live.

BRUTAL BIOLOGY

When the thorny devil feels threatened, it tucks its head between its legs! By doing so, it shows off a very spiny bump on its back, which looks like a false head! This strange body part confuses predators, giving the lizard time to run away.

CHAPTER 5

FEATHERS AND BEAKS

Many vertebrates are covered with scale or hair, but birds are different. They are unique because they have feathers and beaks.

Built to Fly

A bird is built to be light, to help it say in the air. Flight feathers are tough and light, and fit together snugly. That provides a wide surface area for pushing through the air. Most birds have strong flight muscles that move their wings. Some bird bones are hollow, so they weigh very little. Their beaks are light too, far lighter than the jaws and teeth of other animals. Birds that soar and glide, such as vultures and albatrosses, have long wings. Acrobatic birds, such as sparrows have shorter wings. Some birds, such as penguins, cannot fly. Instead, they use their wings to swim speedily through water.

The albatross has the longest wingspan of any bird. It is up to 11 feet (3.4 m) across.

No Fly Zone

The biggest bird in the world is also flightless. It is the ostrich, and it lives in hot **grasslands** and deserts in Africa. The bird has a small head but big eyes and a very long neck—it measures 3 feet (1 m) long. An ostrich moves around on its long, powerful legs. The two feet at the end have enormous claws that can dig up food or slash at predators.

Ostriches lay eggs as big as melons. The chicks that hatch are striped. That makes them difficult for predators to spot in the grass.

BRUTAL BIOLOGY

Ostriches have fluffy white, black, or brown feathers. The feathers are found on most of their body, except for their necks, legs, and under their wings. These areas are bare to help the birds keep cool—heat in blood vessels under the ostriches' skin can escape through the featherless skin.

Big Beak

The shoebill's beak is an enormous body part that looks like the front of a boot or clog. In fact, this remarkable bird's beak is so enormous that the creature is sometimes called the whalehead!

What a Weapon!

The shoebill's beak or bill measures 9 inches (23 cm) long and 4 inches (10 cm) across. It is thick, tough, heavy, and tipped with a nail-sharp hook. The bird stands still on riverbanks in marshlands, where it waits for passing fish, frogs, turtles, snakes, or even baby crocodiles. When it spots its prey, the shoebill attacks fast. It darts its head forward, with its bill open. At the same time, it flaps its wings to keep its balance. Then, the sharp edges of the brutal bill pierce the prey, and grip onto it. Finally, the shoebill swallows its meal.

Shoebills have blue-gray feathers and large, yellow-green eyes.

Adult shoebills can reach heights of up to 5 feet (1.5 m).

Death Nest

A mother shoebill lays two eggs each year, but only one chick survives to adulthood. The chicks hatch with fluffy feathers and cannot fly. They are also too weak to catch their own food until they are more than four months old. The parents bring food to feed both chicks at first, but later, when the chicks are bigger, the parents feed only the larger, stronger one. That is because they cannot catch enough to feed two youngsters. The smaller chick not only gets weaker but also is pecked continually by its bigger brother or sister, and eventually dies.

BRUTAL BIOLOGY

Shoebills nest among grasses at the hottest time of year, when swamplands are driest. The parent birds carry bills full of water to pour over the nests. This keeps the eggs cool, and the chicks inside alive.

Small Bird, Big Beak

All hummingbirds are so-named because their wings make a humming noise as they flap. The wings flap rapidly, as much as 80 times per second! Hummingbirds are small birds with bright feathers, but the sword-billed hummingbird has something that no other bird has—a beak almost as long as its body.

Dig Deep

A sword-billed hummingbird beak is up to 4 inches (10 cm) long, and it uses it to reach deep inside the vine flowers it feeds on. The bird pokes its beak inside a flower to drink the sweet **nectar** within. As it does so, **pollen** from the flower rubs onto the bird's feathers. When the hummingbird visits another flower, the pollen may be left behind, which allows the flower to make seeds.

The sword-billed hummingbird perches with its head pointing upward. It does so to stop it from tipping over!

What a Flight Path!

Feeding inside flowers is precise work, which is why hummingbirds must hover on the spot, fly backward, forward, and even upside-down! Most birds flap their wings up and down, but hummingbirds rotate their wings while moving them forward and backward, making a figure-eight pattern. With this amazing movement, hummingbirds can control their direction with just the slightest twist of their wings.

Flamingos use their large, oddly-shaped beaks to separate mud and food from water.

BRUTAL BIOLOGY

Every beak in the bird family has a shape that is designed for a need. For example, eagles have hooked beaks for ripping flesh, but pelicans have net-shaped bills to scoop up fish. However, some beaks are even more unusual. The flamingo has a boomerang-shaped beak with special grooves along the edge. When the bird plunges its head into water, it takes a big mouthful and uses its strong tongue to push the water out past the grooves. By doing so, it traps tiny shrimps to eat.

CHAPTER 6

MAMMALS ARE AMAZING!

Mammals, including humans, share certain features. Most have hair or fur on their bodies and are warm-blooded. They also feed on their mothers' milk after they are born. The world is full of mammals with amazing anatomies!

The "head finger" parts at the end of an elephant's trunk work like a person's fingers.

Largest on Land

Elephants are the largest land animals on Earth. There are two species of elephant—African and Asian. The African elephant is larger, with bigger ears and a more wrinkled skin. An African elephant's trunk is 6 feet (1.8 m) long, and is like an elongated upper lip and nose. It has nostrils at the end and pointed parts, sometimes called "head fingers," which are used to grip things. The trunk is flexible and strong enough to wrap around and pull down trees, but the head fingers can do delicate tasks, such as cracking open nuts.

Tusks for Every Task

Tusks are special long front teeth. Elephants use them to defend themselves, attack predators, dig, lift objects, and scrape bark off trees. The animals eat bark in the dry seasons, when there are fewer leaves and fruit. Elephants also use their tusks to help them dig water holes in dry riverbeds.

BRUTAL BIOLOGY

The pregnancy of a female elephant lasts for 22 months—longer than any other land mammal. The long pregnancy gives a baby elephant time to grow and develop the brain power it will need to survive. When a baby elephant is born it can weigh more than 250 pounds (113 kg). Baby elephants are called calves.

Elephants can use their tusks to peel off tree bark to eat.

When male giraffes fight, they use their long necks as weapons.

Giant Giraffes

Giraffes are the tallest land animals in the world. They are also one of the most amazing in appearance. Their bodies are covered in beautiful patterns of brown patches, and each giraffe has its very own design.

Amazing Necks

One of the most amazing things about a giraffe's anatomy is its huge neck. A giraffe's neck is 6 feet (1.8 m) long, and is very heavy. Despite the length of their necks, giraffes have only seven **vertebrae**, just like humans. However, the vertebra are much bigger—they can be about 10 inches (25 cm) long. Giraffes use their long necks to hold their heads high in order to spot danger. If they are attacked, they swing their heads against rivals' bodies. They have very strong bones in their skulls to absorb the impact of these blows. Despite that, giraffes can sometimes be knocked out by the blows!

Thorn-Tackling Tongues

Giraffes also use their long necks to reach leaves growing at the top of trees, and then pull off the leaves with their teeth. However, to get leaves from thorny acacia trees, giraffes must reach out their enormous tongues, which can be about 20 inches (50 cm) long. Their tongues are **prehensile**, which means they can curl and wrap around objects and grip them tightly. Giraffes poke their tongues between acacia thorns to grasp and pull off leaves and put them into their mouths.

BRUTAL BIOLOGY

An adult male giraffe's legs alone are 6 feet (1.8 m) long, and at the end of the legs are enormous hooves. Giraffes use their powerful legs to run quickly. They can rush away from danger at a top speed of 35 miles per hour (56 kph).

A large male giraffe can eat as much as 145 pounds (65 kg) of food a day!

Ants for Dinner

The giant anteater is a strange-looking animal. It has a narrow head, long nose, a very long, bushy tail, and large claws that curl under its feet. Although they look unusual, all these features serve a very important purpose—they keep the anteater alive.

Sniff and Eat

As its name suggests, this amazing mammal feasts on ants, but it also eats other insects such as **termites,** too. A giant anteater has tiny eyes and poor sight. It relies on its sense of smell to find food, by sniffing it out. When it finds a nest of insects, the anteater tears into it with its claws. Its rubbery skin and long hair protect it from the bites of angry ants and termites that swarm out of the nest to defend their home.

The thick, bushy hair on an anteater's body protects it in the sun.

A giant anteater can flick its tongue in and out 150 times every minute!

Stick and Scoop

The anteater flicks its long, sticky tongue in and out of the nest to collect food. An anteater's tongue is 2 feet (60 cm) long, and its mouth makes sticky saliva, or spit. Once prey are caught on the tongue, they cannot escape. One anteater can use its tongue to scoop up and eat 30,000 ants in a single day.

BRUTAL BIOLOGY

The armadillo is another strange-looking mammal that, like the anteater, sniffs out insects to eat. It too digs into insect nests with sharp claws. If it is threatened, the three-banded armadillo uses a smart tactic—it rolls up into a ball! The animal is covered with armored, bony plates, which protect its soft body beneath.

Bat wings have bones similar to those found in human arms and hands.

Flying Mammal

Bats are like no other mammal on Earth because they are the only one to have flapping wings and fly! A bat's wings are formed from a double layer of skin that stretches between the sides of the bat's body and the four long fingers on each hand. A bat moves its wing like a hand, which can make it look as if it is swimming through the air. The thumb on each hand is on the front of the wing, and has a claw. The bat uses it to climb up trees, handle its food, and fight.

Hunting with Echoes

The other amazing feature bats have is the ability to hunt and find their way around in the dark using **echolocation**. A bat sends out high, squeaky sounds from its mouth or nose. When the sounds hit an object, an echo comes back. The bat can tell what the object is by the sound of its echo. Most bats hunt for insects, and they can even tell the size, shape, and texture of tiny insects from their echoes.

Deadly Journey

Every year, vast herds of wildebeests travel to find food over very long distances of up to 1,000 miles (1,600 km). This migration starts soon after the calves are born. So, within days, they have to be able to run fast enough to keep up with the herd, which will not stop to wait for calves that fall behind. The herd forges ahead, crossing rivers and lakes in huge numbers. Many calves are injured, lost, drowned, or killed by predators along the way.

BRUTAL BIOLOGY

Fruit bats do not find food using echoes, but instead rely on their amazing senses of sight and smell to track down dinner. The bat also has a very long tongue to help it reach fruit and plant nectar. In fact, the tongue is so long that the bat keeps it rolled up inside, near its ribs, when it is not using it.

Fruit bats have large eyes that work well in dim light, just like those of cats.

CONCLUSION

DESIGNED TO SURVIVE

Extreme animal anatomies are all types of physical **adaptations**. They have developed to help animals find food, a mate, or protect themselves.

Turning into Bats

Amazing adaptations such as the bat's wings developed over many thousands of years. The **ancestors** of bats were tiny mammals that did not have wings. They could not fly, so jumped from tree to tree to catch prey. Those with longer fingers with skin between them found that they could stay in the air for longer. That used less energy than running and jumping between trees. Those bats caught more food, and were better able to survive than other bats. As a result, the bats that descended from them eventually developed wings.

The saiga antelope's large nose is flexible and inflatable.

A World of Adaptation

There are so many examples of amazing animal bodies in our world, from the saiga antelope to the bird of paradise. The saiga antelope's swollen nose has adapted to protect its lungs—in summer, hairs inside filter out dust that could clog up its nose, and in winter the hairs warm the cold air that the antelope breathes in. Birds of paradise have bright, colorful feathers that they use to attract mates in the dim light of their forest homes. Like all other successful animal species, the bodies of these creatures have adapted to survive and thrive on Earth.

BRUTAL BIOLOGY

Today, animals are under threat when they cannot adapt fast enough to the changes humans make to their habitats. Those threats include **habitat** destruction, hunting, and pollution.

Male birds of paradise flash their colorful feathers to attract females to mate with.

GLOSSARY

adaptations the changes in or features of an animal that help it stay alive

ancestors animals in the past from which a modern animal developed

camouflage a color or pattern that matches the surroundings

cocoon the covering some insects make to protect themselves while they develop

constrictors animals that kill prey by squeezing it to death

digests breaks down food inside the body to get nutrients

echolocation the use of reflected sound signals to locate objects or visualize surroundings

exoskeletons skeletons on the outside of the bodies of animals

fins the animal body parts used for steering and swimming

glands body parts that create vital substances, such as venom or sweat

grasslands areas of flat land with mostly grasses and few trees

habitat the environment in which animals and plants live

insects small animals that have six legs and generally one or two pairs of wings

invertebrates animals without backbones

mate to reproduce, or have young

metamorphosis a series of physical changes some animals go through to become adults

nectar the sugary substance found in flowers

organisms living things

paralyze to cause something to be unable to move

pollen a powder made by the male part of a flower

predators animals that catch and eat other animals

prehensile capable of gripping things by wrapping around them

prey an animal that is caught and eaten by other animals

sensory pits dips on the surface of an animal's body that sense heat or electricity

species a type of living thing

tentacles long, flexible arms

termites small, pale, soft insects that live in large colonies

toxic poisonous

tropical describes a region that is very hot because it is close to the equator

venom poison made by animals

vertebrae backbones

vertebrates animals with backbones

warm-blooded describes an animal that has no change in body temperature when its surroundings get colder or hotter

FIND OUT MORE

Books

Earley, Christina. *Adaptations* (Life Science). Crabtree Publishing Company, 2022.

Ganeri, Anita. *Deadly Animals* (Pocket Manuals). Haynes Publishing, 2019.

Spilsbury, Louise and Richard Spilsbury. *Animal Adaptations*. Raintree, 2021.

Websites

Discover more amazing animal senses at:
http://faculty.washington.edu/chudler/amaze.html

Find out more about animal adaptation at:
https://kids.britannica.com/kids/article/adaptation/352704

Learn about incredible Alaskan animal adaptations at:
www.nps.gov/bela/forkids/alaskan-animal-adaptations.htm

Publisher's note to educators and parents:
All the websites featured above have been carefully reviewed to ensure that they are suitable for students. However, many websites change often, and we cannot guarantee that a site's future contents will continue to meet our high standards of educational value. Please be advised that students should be closely monitored whenever they access the Internet.

INDEX

About the Authors

Kelly Roberts is an experienced children's book author who has always been fascinated by the natural world. She has written many science and nature books for children. Louise Spilsbury has written hundreds of children's information books about our natural world.